AS IF THIS DID NOT HAPPEN
EVERY DAY

POEMS BY
PAULA J. LAMBERT

AS IF THIS DID NOT HAPPEN EVERY DAY

POEMS BY
PAULA J. LAMBERT

Sheila-Na-Gig Editions

As If This Did Not Happen Every Day © 2024 Paula J. Lambert

Cover art: Chris Roberts-Antieau, *The Myth of Certainty* (46.75" x 39.5" thread painting and fabric appliqué)
Cover design: Paula J. Lambert
Cover consultant: Ali Wade
Author photo: Paige Critcher

ISBN: 9781962405034
Library of Congress Control Number: 2024936823

Sheila-Na-Gig Editions
Russell, KY
Hayley Mitchell Haugen, Editor
www.sheilanagigblog.com

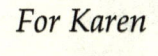

For Karen

Acknowledgments

The following poems were previously published, some in slightly different form, by the following:

Birds of the Cuyahoga: 2022 Edith Chase Poetry Reading Anthology: "Mute"

Braided Way Magazine: "Winter"

Crab Creek Review: "Why Seagull Tries to Eat the Whale When Whale Comes Up to Breathe"

Dissident Voices: A Radical Newsletter in the Struggle for Peace and Social Justice: "Everglades (Burmese Python)"

Gyroscope Review: "Vessel"

Lake Effect: An International Poetry Journal: "This Place, Too, a Loss: Blue Whale"

The New England Poetry Club Online Anthology: "What Grows from a Heart Stopped Cold"

New Verse News: "Just as the Birds, Distracted"

Of Our Own Accord: Anthology of Women's Poetry, Prose, & Art (Flying Ketchup Press): "On the Stories of Spheres (How the World Might Have Turned)"

ONE ART: A Journal of Poetry: "Splendor," "Spring"

Open Air III (OPA Press): "All the Ways We Witness"

Poetic Inventory of the Cuyahoga Valley National Park: "Green Heron"

Sheila-Na-Gig online: "Ars Poetica: Wild Geese," "Revelation: On Watching a Time-Lapse Video of the Ice Sheet Covering Lake Michigan Split in Two and Drift Apart," "Weight"

Silver Birch Press: "Indoctrination, 1972"

Slippery Elm Literary Journal: "The Mechanics of Flight," "Uncanny,"

SWWIM Every Day: "Contrition: Birds-of-Paradise," "Reign of Animals"

2024 Women Artists Datebook (Syracuse Cultural Workers): "Invitation: House Sparrow"

Steam / Sparks / A Thin Stream of Smoke

I remember how much fun it was
        to go to the Richland County Fair,
                to see the steam-powered tractors,

threshers, and sawmills: monsters
        devoted to easing folks' hard work
                and hard living. Monsters that, in the end,

created mountains of work themselves
        and may have been the beginning of
                a certain kind of deadly end. But it was fun

the county fair, especially after dark:
        that's when they added straw to the belly
                of the fires so the monsters blew out sparks:

bright red stars glowing like fireworks
        you could reach out and touch. He used to tell me
                to put his ashes there when he died, blow him out,

too, to the black-night sky, his last-ever spark show.
        No better way to go, he'd laugh, and it was hard
                to argue with that. Years later, still searching

for how to forgive, I settle for seeing the sparks
        of him burning through the night, fading at last
                to a thin wisp of smoke that curls into nothing at all.

This Place, Too, a Loss: Blue Whale

A blue whale's heart, they say,
is big as a Volkswagen Beetle. Because
folks on land, I guess, have no frame of reference
but the cars that carry us through our pitiful days,
place to place, mile after mile,
incessantly searching for something bigger and better
we can call home.

The beat of a blue whale's heart, they say,
can be heard over two miles away, though it's not clear to me
who's listening—a boat, maybe, filled with men
weighed down by sonar devices and plastic coolers,
men with hearts small as a fist—
women, too, maybe, and other folk dreaming
of swimming inside a blue whale's ventricle because

they say that, too, you know,
that the blue whale's arteries are a tunnel
big enough to contain us,
as if that heart, big as a car, beating eight times a minute
and loud enough for most anyone's god to hear, wouldn't burst
our skulls from the eardrums out, drown us in the blood
she's pumping—or trying to, we the clot
most likely to kill her as we breaststroke leisurely
toward the overworked chambers
of her heavy, heavy heart, thinking

this might be it at last. This might be home,
or at least a place we can stay for a while, flip, maybe,
or turn into an Airbnb, somebody else's getaway,
somebody else's home away from home, somebody else's
chance to forget about everything, for a while, till they leave
their two-star review, of course: *seemed spacious*

Wild Ohio: 2023 Edith Chase Poetry Reading Anthology: "Honey Locust Remembers Its Roots," "The Solace of Trying: Bush Honeysuckle"

The author would like to thank the Ohio Arts Council, the Greater Columbus Arts Council, and the Virginia Center for the Arts for their support of her work. She would also like to express her gratitude for the ongoing, loving support of her husband, Michael Perkins.

Contents

I.

II.

III.

*. . . I do not want to say love
is like devouring. But devouring is like love.*

—Danusha Laméris

What Grows from a Heart Stopped Cold

The trumpet vines had taken over the trellis,
wound their way through to the screen porch floor,
walls, roof. I cut it all down.
My daughters didn't talk to me for days.

We had so many hummingbirds then
flitting and buzzing with the fat black bees—carpenters
doing their own damage; I had my reckoning with them, too.

But the scarlet trumpets dangled like candy,
half of the hummingbirds disappearing inside them entirely.
Later,
in less-happy times, I saw a Walton Ford painting:
Limed Blossoms, read about boys chewing wheat paste
to lime the trumpets,
red like these,
so when the birds flung their tongues into the nectary,
ruby-red necks following, just like these, they were
                                   stuck
                                         and died
their terrified hummingbird hearts,
so overworked to begin with,
exploding in fear.

The little boys sold the birds for ladies' hats—
some did it just for fun—either way

the casual cruelty of boys has stopped so many
hearts cold. Yet women bind themselves to them,
         limed
by some invisible force: Scarlet finery, ruby wealth,
                 red necks.

It's a hard world. I've tried to tell the children:
Be careful of what woos you.

Our screen porch now is surrounded by wildflowers:
bee balm, beardtongue, black-eyed Susan. Hedge nettle
and butterfly weed on every corner.

The carpenter bees continue to buzz and thump. I let them.
The hummingbirds have returned, less drunk and dizzy than before,
maybe, less trusting, but hungry, and here,
where a house still stands, awash with color
of every kind, stronger for what was torn from it.

Indoctrination, 1972

You were their leader, that gang of boys, that tangle of freckles
and wide-striped shirts. You chose a girl and they chased her down,

pinning her arms and legs while you kissed her, quick, on the lips.
The day they caught me, I felt a word I couldn't name explode

in my chest. I kicked and scratched at all those hands, those fingers
now losing their grip. You kept coming, leaning in while I lurched

away, until finally letting out a disgusted sigh: *This one's too much*
trouble. Let her go. It was second grade, St. Anthony's school, and

the church loomed, straight and serious, over the playground. At its
entrance, two tall fir trees shivered in the breeze, whispering, laughing.

Why Seagull Tries to Eat the Whale
When Whale Comes Up to Breathe

There is, of course, that mortal thing
that motivates us all: hunger. *Bless us*

O lord, and these thy gifts. But when
the bounty tumbles and rolls through

the sea, islands of trash and fish gut,
when all we see beneath us we believe

is for us, we eat what we will, peckish,
convinced we're starving, believing

we're likely to die. Who but gull was
this sea meant for? Who but gull was

meant for sky, the current of air that
keeps us aloft, alert, rested, cruising

for what wants what we believe is ours?
When the great black mass of the whale

rises, sneaky now, snorkeling, we point
our beaks to the lesions we've caused,

petulant, pathetic, so hungry: eat or be
eaten! And so we eat, and fear, and eat.

Uncanny

I know you know what it feels like, staring
into your phone, bleary-eyed, at 3-or-so'clock
in the morning, trying to fathom the abyss

of what you're witnessing. Charts and graphs
of delusion and disease, primary colors—
primal ones—flipping themselves over

into something you can't make sense of where
red is cold and blue is warm and all you've ever
learned till now has been a conjuring. Earlier,

when you witnessed light bearing down through
darkness—really just a break in the clouds
at an opportune time—and you saw the trees

leaning in to the glow, you knew the moment
held meaning. Tonight, opening the abyss
of pale blue light in your hand, you see maps aflame

with surging cases of COVID-19: counties
where new cases peaked during [orange]
the last week and [red] the last month,

counties where deaths had peaked during
[orange] the last week, and [red] the last month
and staring into chart after chart of the entire

United States pixelated [orange] and [red],
you find yourself staring at the tops of your
comfy, red-leather shoes and neatly folded

bright-orange socks, and the white of your legs
so resonate with the pale green and creamy-white
pattern of your grandmother's kitchen floor.

The cold blue laugh of the boy standing over
you broke into shards and tumbled around
you: *Look at her! Look at those shoes and socks!*

That's when you'd dropped your gaze, seeing
the shoes and the orange socks you'd just put on,
yourself, and the pale-green, creamy-white floor

glistening beneath them seemed to suddenly tilt
sideways. You heard your grandmother's voice
telling the boy *her shoes are fine*, and you heard

something in her voice you'd never heard before.
You never heard Nana sound tired. You never
heard Nana sound frightened. You looked up

to see your grandmother staring not at you or
your shoes but directly at the boy. *They don't match!*
he was yelling again, insistent. *Her shoes and socks*

don't match! Look! And then he lunged, pointing.
You've never stopped looking or hearing those shards
of cacophonous laugh. You've never forgotten

your Nana's intent and questioning stare into his
dark and dagger-like eyes. You've never forgotten
the cold blue light of the open Frigidaire door

behind them. Fifty years later, staring into charts
tracing the path of calamitous illness and death,
you remember the damage that bullies can do.

but not much of a view, and be forewarned
there was some kind of really loud thumping sound
we couldn't find the source of, somebody needs to look into that.
would not recommend, and it seems best for you
to call this place, too, a loss, sell it for what you can get
or maybe just foreclose, maybe just move on.

Weight

In December 2020, Nature *reported that human-made materials weighed 1.1 trillion tons, exceeding the mass of all living things on the planet.*

The weight of steel and concrete, weight
of iron and glass. The weight of streets,

sidewalks, celestial spheres. The weight
of so much grief: populations exploding

while so many species die. The weight
of plastic flamingoes, Tupperware tubs,

swabs, syringes, IV tubes and catheters.
The weight of Band-Aids, diapers, Barbie

dolls and baby dolls. Tonka trucks. Legos.
The weight of home and school, offices

and libraries. Books. The weight of what
we know, the weight of what we wear:

nylon, rayon, Kevlar, spandex. Stretch
denim, wrinkle-free shirts and blouses.

Thong sandals, jelly sandals, eyeglasses,
sunglasses. Prayer beads, prayer rugs,

public art and statuary. Coffee cups and
water bottles. Toilet bowls and toilet brushes,

toothbrushes, hairbrushes, hair pins,
headbands. The miles of tiles underground,

so many miles of trenches. Dump trucks,
bulldozers, city buses, cars. Tanks, guns,

missiles. Ships and sail boats, life preservers.
Fishing poles and fishing line. Kite string,

kites. What we make to measure wind.
The scales we use to measure weight itself.

How we love to know things, make things,
measure things, kill things. How we love

to eat. How little we complain of the weight
we ask the Earth to bear. How much we keen

for what we still don't have, the gnawing
weight of hunger, the endless need for more.

Spring

The strange beast of the night
has retreated, hackberry down,
no more damage than that
and the echoing tinnitus you woke with,
b-flat, constant, dull.

The wind's wild paw —
which took out a city west of here —
left the fence intact. Small favor.
Elsewhere, children are dead.
The storm, sure. The anguished shooter.
Pockets of silence everywhere,
in the aftermath. You calculate:

chainsaw, chipper, enough mulch
to cover the peonies, the lilacs,
the hydrangea and rose of Sharon
sure to follow.

They won't ever say they were sorry; they won't
ever say they were wrong. Their voices get louder
and louder, and they just keep blaming you.

And in these charts you see the beauty of orange
and red and how they're working together.
You admit when you first saw the charts you saw

fire, thought they were tracing fire itself—and
in a way, they were—but then you saw the beauty
of clarity blazing. You thought of the trees

you saw earlier, leaning toward the light: *Give
me some more,* said the trees, *Let us drink it all in,*
said the trees. And you understood the uncanny,

beautiful way those trees had glowed. The angry
boy grew up, went away, and died. You grew up,
went away, and, somehow, keep living.

There's no sense, really, to the living and dying,
all that anger and hurt. Some of us are born
with eyes wide open. Some of us die refusing to see.

Some of us never stop staring into our phones,
or writing down what we think we remember,
trying to make sense of color and pattern, memory

and meaning, love and fear and light waving
through trees, sometimes shining through, sometimes
bursting, sometimes burning everything down.

Honey Locust Remembers Its Roots

Honey locust leafs out late in spring
while strongly scented, cream-colored
flowers produce the pods that mature

in autumn. Herbivores eat the pulp
and excrete the seeds now fertilized
by their droppings. Honey locust,

invasive, a nuisance, a pest, has thorns
up to four inches long that evolved
to protect them from animals

now extinct: Pleistocene megafauna
hunted by humans who evolved
themselves to use the thorns for nails,

timber for rails resistant to rot, pods
for medicine and tea. Humans came
to tame the wild, and trees capable

of fending off mammoths were bred
instead to ornamentals, thriving
where few other trees could prosper,

able to survive heat and drought and
transplant, compacted soil, housing
developments and all those brand-new

neighborhood parks. Honey locusts,
yellow-gold, delicately dropping their
feather-like leaves through crisp autumn

afternoons, drowse through the dark,
dreaming of what they once were—
and still are, some places: aggressive,

invasive, choking waterways and
harboring vermin while thorns, clustered
like claws, keep looming beasts at bay.

Everglades (Burmese Python)

And so, I missed my chance with one of the lords
Of life. —D.H. Lawrence

They killed her, of course.
It was what they'd set out to do.
Invasive.
Renegade.
The actual stuff of nightmares.

Her final meal
was a white-tailed deer. Three men,
it took, to wrangle her. She didn't go down easily.
For all their manpower, still she managed
to slap one upside the head with her tail.

Wouldn't you, I wondered,
fight like hell after so many years
of surviving in a place you never wanted to be?
Wouldn't you devour every single thing in your path?
Wouldn't you make plans for your progeny
to strike fear in the hearts of men—

men making plans of their own,
sending horny male *scouts*
fitted with radio transmitters and looking for mates
into the swamp, leading the charge
to search and destroy the females?

All I can think is that she survived,
and fiercely, all these goddamned years.
Eighteen-feet long,
two-hundred-and-fifteen pounds,
carrying one hundred twenty-two eggs.
It's just next-level for us, they said.

Bigger than anyone knew.
Breaking every record they had.
Multiplying in ways they hadn't been able to fathom.

Ten thousand more, they warn the world,
are out here, in the *Lake of the Holy Spirit,*
this *River of Grass,*
these *grassy waters* going on forever.

Reign of Animals

In Texas, fish pelted the pavement,
less stunned than the men who found them
in the parking lot. They'd come a long way,
the fish. It was a hell of a ride, lifted from the sea
by a force no fish brain could possibly have fathomed,
slapped down dead at the used car dealership
on Summerhill Road. The men who gathered,
trying to figure out what in the name of sweet baby Jesus
could have happened, were at a disadvantage,
never having been lifted themselves, knowing plenty
about plagues of frogs and locusts but next to nothing
about fishes come without loaves. They'd heard
that crack of thunder, five days past Christmas,
two days before the new year. *Fish were dropping*
here and everywhere, they'd told the reporter,
not knowing what to say except what was obvious,
broken fish bodies starting to stink up their shoes.
The smell stayed with them all day, and now,
after saying prayers and shivering in the cold
that came with the storm, they stared at the ceiling
wishing there'd been a way to close those damn
fish eyes staring like they'd seen the face of God.
And they guessed the fish had. And they guessed
that was blasphemy. And they guessed the fish
had gotten what they deserved. So they closed
their own eyes and curled up closer to their wives,
women who'd been staring at the ceiling for weeks,
who were pretty sure they knew what those fish
had been through, pretty sure they hadn't seen God.

The Way of the World Seems Clear

The way of the world seems clear
as the heron stabs the fish
and stabs him again
and again
and as she lifts him in her beak
and opens her beak unfathomably wide
and opens her throat
unfathomably

so the fish's broad tail,
strange signpost to the last of the fish's existence,
vanishes down the distorted gullet and into the oblivion

of the bird's belly.
(Smaller fish, swallowed without the stabbing,
swallowed whole and alive, die inside
as we all do, watching.)

And when the bird lifts the weight of her body —
now with the weight of the fish's body —
into the air, rising above the water's mirrored surface
(the bird's reflection,
the sun's,
the sky's)

we call this heron *a holy spirit*,
the clouds on the surface of the water *a miracle*,
the bob and weave of shadows swimming below
part of the circle of life.
What is.
What feeds.
What keeps us alive.

I am thinking now
Of grief, and of getting past it

—Mary Oliver

Splendor

The fig wasp, born pregnant,
offers herself back to the fig
and dies. My every day feels like this:
clambering out of my dreams, laden,
flitting about the world
collecting what the earth and air offer—
sunlight, the vast blues and linen whites of sky
(some days, only moist air and gray
all around me), the pain of purpled iris
exploding from the tips of their slender green spears.

I never asked for this life, what it gives,
what it takes away,
its every moment of cruelty
and joy. Still, I move through the day
greedy with want,
aching with what must be love—
what other word for this pull to return
to the slim cavern of sleep that,
entering, takes my wings
and shreds my senses
into the crazed stomping
of my daily death, letting go
of everything this day has burdened me with
and sleeping—truly, like the dead—
then waking, laden with more.

Just as the Birds, Distracted

Most nights this week, there will be more birds in the air above
this country than people in beds down below. —Josh Sokol

Just as the birds, distracted by light
that splits the star they follow into sparks
and mirrors so they never see the towers
that reach out to kill them, just as the birds,

so entranced by needs they cannot explain
that they propel themselves steadfastly
forward through all the wildfires we set
for them (if they recognize their own

plummeting numbers when they emerge
from the smoke, they don't show it,
they keep flying), just as the birds
soar even through their own sleep

as, one by one by one, they die of thirst
or starvation or exhaustion, falling into fields
and ditches and sidewalks, mountain peaks
and seldom-seen valleys, just as they

keep going, season after season, year after
year, eon after unfathomable eon, so we
in our beds below sleep through it all,
writhing maybe through tangles of sheets

and the existential threat we've made
of our lives—we who've lived long enough
to multiply every problem we inherited,
who've ignored or angrily explained away

the desperate patterns of our own migration—
but sleeping, blithely unwilling to do more
than worry while, awake, we grab our keys
and cameras and binoculars and go

to the marshes, waterways, and wild places
still left, still untrampled, still—unbeknownst
to us—part of the twisted dreams and difficult
truths we rarely remember, come morning.

All the Ways We Witness

Migrating songbirds that vocalize, or call, at night during
their flights are far more likely to strike buildings than
those that are silent. —audubon.org/news

Stay silent and stay your course, my friend.
True north. Call no one toward your purpose.

Let white-throated sparrow sing, and thrush,
and warbler, through the crystal forest light.

Let them crash, and die, and let their bodies
be counted. That's witness, too, to the hands

that hold them. Let silence be your witness,
and darkness, and your wild, willing flight.

Mute

What (else) might we learn from the swan so-named
for the silence of its flight,
no honk or hiss, no call or song,
no sound but the earnest beat of its wings…

Moon, and Earth, and Home

In the dream we watched the moon, enormous
and shining white before us, and as we watched,
the mottled gray of its surface became the earth

reflected, black and white, still so big and very,
very bright. When you asked me where I lived,
I pointed to the second story of a building

beside us: *There.* You held my hand and moved it,
still pointing, down the row of windows overhead
till we came to one unlit and said, *No. We live here.*

Invitation: House Sparrow

From the next room, I heard what I couldn't
identify, a kind of clawing. I found the bird

in the dining room window, beak entrenched
in the threads of the screen, neck wrenching

with determined thrust as she yanked what
she needed for her nest. My own jaw dropped

wide open, so surprised by the perfect square
of the hole that framed her, the strength of her

every twist and pull. I swear, when she saw me
she was angry, eyes flashing black light,

the top of her head dark as a bruise against
the brown of her body: *Who are you to intrude?*

Mind your business. In another flash, barely
seeming to move at all, she glared at me

from a branch full of blossoms in the pear tree
three feet away, defiant, daring me to stop her.

One house builds another. She offered the gift
of her need. Who was I, indeed, to refuse it?

Contrition: Birds-of-Paradise

Though pelts had long been traded across Asia, wings and feet removed,
Europeans first encountering Birds-of-Paradise believed the birds must have
floated on air until, like exhausted angels, they simply fell to earth.

You did not fall, dear heart. We reached for you and,
so surprised our human hands made contact,
pulled you down to what could only be your hell.

Bless us, oh beautiful bird, wingless, footless,
still carrying the scent of cinnamon, cloves, and greed,
for we have surely sinned, so many times

and in so many gruesome ways. We failed to see you,
holy relic, as witness to our own hubris, our inability
to understand that reaching was its own gift.

Oh, beautiful bird, we see you now and bow to you,
ask you to believe we of featherless form can do better,
can be better — truly and without irony —

than what our fathers taught us. We reach now only
for your forgiveness, understanding our penance at last
and firmly resolving, with the help of your grace,

to amend our lives and to see your lovely, still-living
progeny for what they are: testament to what we might
be instead of what we might own.

When the Strands of Our Stories Are Woven Together, They Vibrate, and Maybe That Means We're Never Alone

I. Passion: Nikola Tesla

One day, missing from a meeting
where he was about to be awarded a medal,
Nikola Tesla was found in Bryant Park.
He stood, arms outstretched, crowned
and covered in birds, a sea of birds at his feet.

Later, when the bird he loved most
came to tell him she was dying,
he said the light that shone from her eyes was dazzling:
a light more intense than any he'd produced
in his lab. I loved her, he said. I understood her,
and she understood me. When the light went out of her eyes,
the light went out of his life. Tesla's birds
followed him everywhere: into and out of hotel rooms,
converging in Bryant Park. Tesla kept every window open,
closing more and more doors.

Born in a storm as lightning flashed,
called by his mother a child of light, Tesla said
he wanted to harness the power of nature.
He went on to mesmerize the world
until, out west, he started a fire
that burned his lab to the ground. After that,
it was harder and harder to find the light,
but he found himself drawn more and more to the birds
who flew to his window to be fed—or sometimes, injured,
to be healed. They left their droppings behind
so hotel maids and managers flew into rage,
one after another insisting he leave until, at last,
Tesla died, penniless, alone, the dreams and drawings left behind

foreshadowing what was to come: radio waves
and wireless transmission, cell phone towers and birds —
oh, our bright and beautiful, dazzling birds —
dying and dying and dying.

II. Indifference: Jersey City, NJ

It was meant to be dignified,
news reports said. *A flock of doves*
soaring majestically past the skyline.
But the Jersey City 9/11 Memorial Committee waited too long,
every professionally trained dove sold
for the other Memorials planned.

Desperate, stupid, hungry to finish the job,
the committee chief thought of the poultry market in Newark
and purchased eighty squabs. Those birds,
who'd never seen the sky, released from the cages
they'd lived in all their tender lives, fell to the river,
bounced against buildings, crashed
into the already-grieving crowd.
They were soup birds, said the chief.
I like the idea that I helped them,
that I got them another chance.

And he wasn't really wrong.
The injured birds gathered were treated.
The ones who figured out how to flap their wings
and fly through the rest of the ceremony — which went on,
mind you, *a blur of feathers and confusion* — figured out later
how to feed themselves, scavenging scraps
like other survivors before them,
like all the survivors who followed.

III. Fly Guy: a Hell of a Thing

I'm sure that one pigeon story
has nothing to do with the other. I'm sure
that Tesla was mad, the man in New Jersey overworked
and underpaid. I'm sure that the bird Tesla loved
had nothing to do with bird populations today,
and even that the squabs sold in the markets
are nothing more or less than delicious.

But I also know this: that the *tesla*—
a unit of magnetic attraction—can explain
the pull of the earth, as well as the strength of the stars.
We are held together like stars, said Tesla,
though the ties cannot be seen.

And it's a hell of a thing
that the head of the Jersey City 9/11 Memorial Committee
went to prison, years later, for nothing to do with the birds
but was promptly christened "Fly Guy,"
that he was good with his hands and repairing transistor radios
so the guards could listen to music,
that he was actually a great musician,
so the prisoners formed a band, and when he got out
he kept making music, and he organized charities
to benefit shelters for penniless men who had nowhere else to live.
He decided to *work with his mind*, and developed a wireless app
that would transmit video surveillance
to the cops who'd put him in jail.

IV. Hindsight: A New Kind of Light

When the strands of our stories are woven together
they vibrate, and maybe that means nothing at all,
but it's nice to think that something is holding us all

together, pulling us all together, and it's nice to think we can fall in love
with the birds—or at least care enough about them
to find out if they can fly before tossing them off a building—
and it's nice to think that's enough:
to keep birds and people out of cages, making music instead,
or sending out signals that help us keep an eye on each other
so when somebody shows up missing somebody else can find them,
covered in what they love,
and when somebody does something stupid,
they might get a second chance. We might all get a chance
to discover a new and dazzling kind of light: that birds understand
more than we'd realized, that every love is true,
that none of us have ever really been lost or forgotten,
that the strands of our lives made sense all along.
That we and the bright and beautiful birds
don't have to die, that we all can go on living
and living and living.

How to Trust the Moon (Chicken)

Why did the chicken cross the road?
Because Chicken saw something fit to pursue. Chicken yearns,
and his commitment to what he yearns for is steadfast.
Maybe some sweet hen—maybe a rooster. Maybe a future,
or a chance to escape the farmer's ax.

Chicken's eyes are always ahead of his gait:
head thrusts forward, long neck locks into place,
and while his vision comes fully into focus,
one foot follows another, catching up.

The better question, maybe, is why Chicken
didn't look back. Why no one taught him what a boundary was,
or that journeys like his have consequences.
Maybe Chicken, spared of the ax—
who may have left hen and a couple of eggs behind—
saw only the sun rising and falling
and wanted to know where it went. Maybe he saw the moon
and dreamt the word *derivative*. Maybe he woke afraid.
Maybe he saw the greener pasture,
luxury condos, a convertible passing him by,
but listen:

Chicken's eyes are stuck in their sockets.
His brain extends to his neck. Had he not escaped the farmer's ax,
he might still have crossed that road.
He might have remembered a former life, some part of his past
he couldn't quite grasp: tsunami's wave heaving skyward,
earth giving way beneath his feet, the scream of a siren
right when the world went black.

Ask this: how life propels him forward.
Why he goes—and keeps going, despite the roar of doom and terror

that hits him along the way. How he follows the light
where it lands. How to trust the moon and why,
when he so often wants to cry, he so often laughs instead.

On the Stories of Spheres
(How the World Might Have Turned)

It was Ptolemy who told us to cast our wishes
on falling stars, as it meant that, in their boredom,

the gods were also curious and so peeked down
through the spheres. Stars tumbling through gaps

they pulled in that strange curtain were a sign
the gods were listening. The story of the spheres

seems strange tonight, election eve, as I watch
the just-past-full Blue Moon rise through the sky.

I don't know that much, really, about Ptolemy
or gods so bored by their own creation. I do know

something of the moon and her names: Flower,
Wolf, Strawberry, Harvest. Even Blue Moon

can be counted on to keep her steady watch, as if
lighting our way was all she was ever meant for.

Syntaxis Mathematica, later called *Almagest,*
was compromised of thirteen books, and it lasted

over twelve hundred years as model of the universe.
One wonders how the world might have turned if,

in all that time, we had focused more on the Moon
and on those who called her by her thirteen names.

Uncertainty: Starlings

I.

Once, on retreat in Amherst, Virginia,
I watched the starlings sweep and fold the sky
at exactly five o'clock every day. *Day is done!* called the birds.
Dinner waits! And the poets, painters, and composers
opened their doors, sauntering down the lane.
While there, I communed
with the vultures every morning,
and one afternoon heard a hawk that wasn't a hawk
at all—just a blue jay guarding its nest.
Maybe the hawk
that bothered the jay was the same bird of prey
that chased those starlings home. Really, while I was there,
the center was a symphony of birds.
I wrote them all
down.

II.

In Denmark,
where the number of starlings
is vast, murmurations are called *Sort Sol*.
Just past sunset, when the starlings start to swarm,
hundreds of thousands of birds—a half million, a million—
search for a place to roost.
The sky goes fully dark.
Should a goshawk enter the flock, the birds start to shit and vomit
till the predator, feathers laden with the sticky weight
of the birds' refusal, turns back
or falls to the sea
and drowns.

III.

There's not always
safety in numbers, though that's the reason
the star-speckled birds swoop and glide in nearly perfect unison.
The falcon cannot focus on his prey
if the starlings rise and glide
as one.
On a December day
in Ferrol Spain, starlings fell
from the sky, pelting cars and people on their way down.
Witnesses said *it sounded like thunder.*
News reports called it
a gruesome sight.
Experts surmised it was electrocution,
not uncommon in close formations, one wing brushing
a high-voltage cable sending current through
to the rest. A month before,
in Anglesey, Wales,
two hundred starlings died
in a dive formation: *a miscalculation*
experts called it there. The far end of the flock
smashed into a country lane. *Blunt force trauma*, inspectors said.
A common thing — it happens
all over the world.

IV.

In Virginia,
writing through hunger
I was trying so hard to explain, hoping the vultures would help,
I'd not expected the starlings to intervene,
to call me away from my work,
luring me,
like the blue jays, away

from what, perhaps, I was not prepared
to encounter.

V.

Starlings talk, you know.
They imprint, and they pick up human speech.
Mozart kept one as a pet. When it died, he wrote this poem
for the funeral: *Here rests a bird called starling / foolish little darling.*
Still in his prime / when he ran out of time....
You get the idea.
But the starling helped him compose
Piano concerto No. 17, in G. Mozart whistled to the bird and listened
when the bird sang back. Even when the bird sang sharp
he wrote it all down, added flute and oboe,
bassoon and strings and
horns, keeping track
of every note.

VI.

In Ancient Rome,
Augurs studied the patterns
of murmuring starlings to divine the will of the gods.
Did they ever see
lightning
strike the flock? Or watch the birds rise
more wide than high so part of it crashed to the ground?
There were so many starlings then. The oracles cared less about birds
than the soldiers headed to battle,
and less for them
than the king
they wanted to please. What would happen if they called it
wrong? In truth, because the augurs could not control
the starling some of them turned to chickens

instead, withholding food
then scattering it,
watching them scratch and feed.
Then they told the king
their lies.

VII.

Starlings stick together
to keep an eye on their own. Each bird
watches seven others — that's it — and the formation rarely falters.
Even so, in Spain, the air itself, mesmerized,
couldn't keep them aloft.
And in Wales,
a place where starlings are sacred,
where a bucolic country lane seemed suddenly a hammer,
the spirit of Branwen wept again with the wind.
Birds know grief, and they understand
fear. But they also fly
in the face of it,
outwitting
what wants to hurt them,
waltzing with each other. Mozart's starling lived with him, alone,
three years. The starling helped him
grieve. When the bird passed away —
perhaps of a grief of its own — Mozart planned the funeral
he couldn't attend for his father. *Opera buffo*:
life itself is absurd.
In Virginia,
newly afraid of the dark, I watched the sky
each afternoon waiting for light to die. The starlings came instead
and, suddenly, doors opened. I wasn't alone.
I followed my hunger
home.

VIII.

This is important to know:
in Denmark, where the sheer number of murmuring starlings
is startling, where the number might lead us
to think the sky will pulse like this
forever,
the numbers themselves—
the mass of birds who, remember, want only
to be safe enough to roost, to sleep and to dream themselves—
are deceiving. Once, the starlings there
filled the skies every day,
all year. Now,
the flocks are fleeting.
The starlings left keep moving,
searching for each other. There are more starlings
in Rome than there were
when Augury
was sacred.
The Romans *tsk* and grunt
as they raise umbrellas—their shield against the sky—warding off
exactly the stank that fell the northern goshawk.
And in places like Virginia,
starlings are maligned…
or murdered.
Invasive,
they never actually invaded,
or asked to come at all. They crossed the sea in a cage.
Set free in Central Park, all they did was
thrive, still searching
for their sisters.

IX.

Our place in the world has always been

uncertain. We were never meant to outnumber starlings,
to outnumber the stars on their backs.
But here we are, loving the birds
and blaming the birds
for what we see when we know: like us,
the birds are dying.
Like us,
the birds are trying
to keep themselves aloft. What's left for us all
but to stick together, to sing and to soar where we are, when we can.
To let the food we find pass through us.
To trust the sky and rise.
To rise and rise
again.

The Limb

My fear is that you'll look up one day
and see all that you've missed. I fear that

more than you not looking up at all, and
never knowing, and never changing

your ways—you'll have to do all this all
over again, you know. It's seeing that

saves us. Here, I want to say *and all*
the hard work that comes, after. But it isn't

work, is it, so much as letting go: a bird
who thinks too much will never lift off

the branch. Bird has only to look up, see
the sky and know her place in it. Then,

it's as if the branch had never existed at all
and also like it had been there all along.

Oh, my sisters.
You never had to be perfect.

—Sakula

Winter

In Wellfleet Bay, cold-stunned turtles
drift on the surface of the sea, Christ-like,
no less miraculous. We're due for this lesson:
slowing down when we feel overwhelmed.
Stopping is an answer if only because
it's all we can do. Wait to be rescued.
Dark shadows patrolling the shore need
to believe they can do some good.
What is the sea, otherwise, but the crash
and roar of abyss beside them—what, even,
the cold light of dawn without the weight of
something with a heart still beating, still
breathing in their hands, something they can
save, and set on its way, that they, too,
now multiplied, can go on.

Molt/What We No Longer Need

In a past life, I was murdered by a man
who left me in a ditch to die. Once, in this life,
I was loved by a man who nearly killed my spirit.
In a future life, I'd like to live like a lobster
shedding every shell that surrounds me
as I grow just a little bit bigger,
as I grow just a little bit wiser.

(Do you know the lobster puffs herself up
when she molts? That, hiding naked and afraid,
she swells to the size she needs her next shell to be?)

(And do you know that hermit crabs leave the shell they outgrow
for smaller crabs to find?)

(And do you know the Monarch caterpillar
suffers five molts—*five*—before the chrysalis? That after
the chrysalis, after the exhaustion of wrenching
herself out of that casing, she gives herself time
to stretch and dry and tentatively flutter
those strange, glorious wings?)

Over and over and over again, in the vast terror-filled beauty
of the universe, we surround ourselves
with what we need to protect ourselves.
And when, sooner or later, we shed the shell that binds us,
we grow into what comes next.

Silt

a golden shovel, after Adelaide Simon's "Panther"

The way of the world is slow but sure. Silt
gives in to freefall, lets itself go where water is
bound, down, ever down, and in its falling
remembers the stone it was, hard and
unyielding, until the glaciers spread, the
wind roared, and finally, finally, river
carried what was left. Silt knows life grinds
us into what we were meant to be, slowly
and fiercely tearing at all that held us down.

On Watching a Time-Lapse Video of the Ice Sheet Covering Lake Michigan Split in Two and Drift Apart

Something in the silence of it all—
      the clean break, the quiet cleaving,
            ice bereft of ice, the slow drifting,

the slow relief   release   slow
      dawning: breakthrough, breaking
            apart, breaking away, the shadow's lean

and reach, the new and different light,
      the final, golden revelation:
            was there, in the beginning, a low

creaking moan, a sudden screeching
      crack in this undoing? And, below,
            did they blink and stretch and celebrate

this dawning light, mouths agape?
      Did they swim toward it or away,
            welcome it or fear it, or—in their usual

hunger—shrug it away? Are they
      like us, the fish, the lampreys,
            the mussels and sunken ships—

did they see it as if for the first time,
      as if it were new, and we were, as if
            this did not happen every moment

of every day, every year, every time:
      cold hearts breaking and opening
            and revealing, and then, somewhere,

closing again? As if this were not
      what life is, what love is, as if this
            were not what you are, what I am.

The Way of the World Seems Clear (II)

The way of the world seems clear
as the fish glides through the water
and sees, too late,
the heron's yellow leg and then—
well, perhaps—
the face of some fish god.
And as the water, clouded with bubbles and debris, clears.
And as the current keeps on.

Waning Gibbous

My poet friends are posting
about the Full Worm Moon.

One day past. I'm late
to every party—late to rage,

late to grief, late to joy and
laughter. Today, Sun outdid

himself, shining so brightly.
He still couldn't warm us.

Spring likes to taunt. Nothing
new, not even this year. Truth

told, we like the taunting: hide
and seek, show and tell,

whack-a-mole. Crocus. Tonight,
dark and cold, I got up, finally,

from the sofa to draw the blind,
and there she was: high, white,

unperturbed. Cold. I know this
love, the kind that says, *I'm here*

always. That's enough. It's what
I can do. And it is enough. It is

tonight. Because I'm tired, too,
and I know the shine can be

exhausting. A thousand nights
I'd prefer only that she be here.

It's a lot for her, and it's enough
for me, the distant, tender wane.

Green Heron

It's been hard for me to love Green Heron.
Homely, hidden, hardly moving at all, staring
into the depths, eyes made for that staring,

pointed permanently down, as if Sky never
mattered at all. How often we lift our eyes
to see her sisters soar: Great Blue, Egret,

those of the graceful glide, the long necks,
long legs, all while Green Heron hunches,
staring ever down, easy to overlook, so easy

not to see at all until she springs to action—
even then, we question what we've seen.
Praise the eater and the eaten, Joy Harjo says.

Praise beginnings; praise the end. Praise
our eyes now opened, praise understanding.
Praise the serpentine neck, suddenly retracted

and hidden again. Praise the fish swallowed.
I am the fish, writes Mary Oliver, *the fish
glitters in me; we are risen, tangled together,*

certain to fall back to the sea. Bless Green Heron
and her quietude. Bless beak become spear,
the javelin thrust. Bless homeliness, and bless

what it hides—bless all that it provides. Bless
the depths reflected, mirrored sky, the bird who
watches and who sees, bless the un-beautiful

creatures so quick to judge. Bless ignorance,
and patience, and forgiveness, and love. Bless
every new beginning. Bless everything that ends.

When the Seas Were Silent

Measure the walls. Count the ribs. Notch the long days.
—Dan Albergotti

When the seas were silent, the whales
rejoiced. I know that joy, those waves

of relief, the flood of absence. Purity.
The rise of your own breath. Last night,

I dreamt of being truant from school
then returning. I couldn't get used to

the sound and rhythm of my classmates,
so I wandered off alone. An old woman,

white-haired, watched me, wanting to
tell me what I didn't have time to learn.

I had to be back in class where we all
lay down on the floor together, a sea

of bodies writhing. I was sick with touch
and noise and laughter till I recognized

the boy beside me. He leaned in, let me
press myself against him till I calmed.

Then I levitated above the bob and sway
of bodies still laughing, reached down

to press the palm of my hand to the head
of a boy below me. *Stop*, I said. *Stop*.

Then I woke to a sea of no-sound, tense,
waiting. The whales knew and I know:

it will all come back. This week, a friend
found a whale, hand-carved, broken

in two, in a trash can. She brought it
home to mend, but the curve of its tail

wouldn't rejoin his body. Strangely,
someone showed her another whale

broken at the same slender curve,
where whale becomes tail, where—

if the whale were real—it would have
writhed itself forward through the sea.

The same place, I realize now, that
my spine turns into tail, the part of me

aching for days as we've all been
inoculating, preparing to return to

a waiting sea-world of blaring sound
and noxious sea-traffic. I just don't

want to go. Like whales stunned by joy
when ships were bound to the bay,

I felt myself free in the void of a viral
world, a world I knew how to navigate.

My friend, buoyed by so many wanting
to see the whale made whole, tried again

to save it and did. When the epoxy dried,
she cradled it to her chest and smiled.

It made me believe the world might be
willing to hold me, like that, like the boy

I'd dreamt of, able to calm me through
a school of bodies touching and being

touched everywhere, loud, laughing,
silly with joy and with love, unmoored.

What I Know Now

Shall I tell you the vision I had
of the blue tongues gathered
in a cosmic circle, one tongue

turning to lick me, to enter me,
rising through my chakras
till the crown convulsed, ready

to burst back into stars? Shall I
tell you of the blue tongue sliding
its way back down, my third eye

throbbing, throat pulsing, belly
burning, the tongue then licking
what it licked when it entered

till that part of me quivered in
ecstatic joy? Would it shock you
to know this vision helped me

understand *The Ecstasy of
St. Theresa*, rendered in marble
by Bernini, angel before her

wielding a tongue of its own?
*The soul is satisfied now with
nothing less than God*, she wrote.

What did I know of tongues and
God when I first saw her writhing,
rising through something solid

as stone? When the blue tongue
that blessed me retreated, I turned
into tongue myself and joined

the others, completing the cosmic
circle, the tips of all our tongues
stretching to meet in the middle,

then touching, center exploding into
sparks as pure and white as the stone
I'd feared all souls were made from.

Vessel

You hold my hips in your hands
and drink. I am a bowl, a chalice,

Moon sending down silver light.
You are the earth and so thirsty.

Ars Poetica: Wild Geese

after Mary Oliver

If I said each bird I've used in a poem was a symbol
for something else — that preening was a metaphor,
or hatching, or hefting a seed
in a beak specifically designed for that purpose —

do you see how the logic might offend the birds
themselves? How it condescends

even to humans
who ought to be better at seeing what the world lays bare
before us? We aren't, of course. That's why it's so tempting

to burden the birds with being more than they are,
something meant to teach us, or sustain us,

to say even the sky must stand for something else,
freedom, maybe — which, nowadays,
does feel like a lofty ideal, something out of reach,
something that, however we might aspire to it,
slips through our fingers,
illusion, a meanness,
not-there-at-all.

The sky's not even blue, you know.

We are, often enough.

And if sky's not there, were the geese I heard honking
this morning — and I mean, *loud,* so I looked up to watch them pass —
just a dream, after all? Something I'd conjured?

But that might be me asking you if the geese were more
than geese, or less than,
and we're right back where we started. What burden

do I place on birds for writing them down
when I only just happened to overhear them?
　Still,
they were *extraordinarily* loud, the geese,
and they did seem to call to me
as much as to each other. I lifted my eyes

and whatever spirit is really *did* seem to soar
inside me.
And by that logic, the wild geese did offer themselves

to my imagination
and yours.

And it might be we're meant to be lifted
by the birds: passerines, waterfowl, raptors. We might be
meant to lift each other. The geese have a long way to go
and might have been showing off.
I might have been part of what kept them awake
or kept them believing they could achieve their impossible journey.
Best, maybe, to see the birds as birds
and as something more. Best, maybe,
to see the world that way
and keep writing it all down. Best
to see this poem as something more than a poem.

Refusing to Give

When the weather is gray and gray
and gray and gray—no rain, which
you might have called a blessing,
or a baptism, or a nourishing—

when all seems stillness—moisture
hanging in the air, blessings held
back, a cold shoulder refusing
to forgive, refusing to give,

when this veil before the light
obscures everything you've ever
found beautiful: maple leaf in free fall,
maple herself revealing more sky,

when dull grass swells with what
it's gathered from the air, this
not-rain you've mourned for days.

when this gray, this gray, this
expansion of nothing and everything
all at once, all around you, this gray
and gray and gray and gray, this

promise, this holding, this shielding
from all that's been too bright,
too fire-bright to witness, too much,
too much, too much terrible light
for our willful, tired eyes . . .

when you see, at last, this gray, this
gray, this damp and nourishing gray,
this vast and empty gray, this holding
on, this holding us, this, holding us
through everything.

Daffodil

I thanked the bloom this morning
as I snipped the base of her stem.

Truth is, I'd not asked if she were
willing to be taken inside, willing

to brighten my table, willing to trade
wind and sun, the coming rain, for

my simple vase, water from the tap,
a pinch of sugar and my distracted

adoration. Defiant, long stem naked
in the glass, she stands tall and turns,

just slightly, away from me. I allow
her that dignity and turn away, too,

sunlight sliding through the blinds,
lingering in the lines between us.

The Solace of Trying: Bush Honeysuckle

Every spring I gather gloves and tools,
    load the wheelbarrow, head out to face
        the clambering honeysuckle once more.

Every spring, a new section of the yard,
    a new line of defense, wrestling despair over
        what comes at us in waves we can't beat back—

not in time. Already there's a tangle
    of overgrowth snaking through my ankles
        as I scour the branches for birds' nests.

Still early. Still safe. But I startle
    at the height of these slender, budding
        shoots, what's risen straight up through

the wild mess below, so anxious
    to pay homage to the sun, to drink it all in,
        green heads shrieking toward the light while

so much dead brittle brush crackles
    beneath my boots. So often this seems
        the legacy of my life: to have failed. But

there's solace in trying, in the lessons
    of witness and feeling yourself helpless,
        plowing through anyway and suddenly seeing

new green thumbs—daffodils—blushing
    toward light meant for them all along. You'll say
        it's too much, but I swear to you, they smile.

Turtle

for W.L.

I.

It was a long time ago.
I've written about it before,
that turtle in my rear-view mirror
spinning away from my car
like a lost hubcap.
What was I to do, so late for work,
so many students waiting?

Later, a few weeks,
a few months—who knows?
Another turtle, smashed
on the side of the road.
Different road, different county.
I on my bike this time, pedaling away

and away and away from my home
every afternoon. I learned
the smell of death that summer:
opossums, birds, this turtle
still alive, trying to retreat
into a shell smashed into itself,
pieces a bloody roadmap
of its stunted life—and mine.
Turtle said, *This is what you did.*
Look close so you won't forget
I, too, had someplace to go.

II.

A friend tells me a dream
he's had all his life. He's a boy
wearing a mask wherever he goes.
Can you see the mask? I ask.
He smiles shyly and nods:
I see it. It's a turtle.

III.

Not long ago, I learned
a turtle's shell is not the little hat of a home
I'd always assumed. It's skeleton —
part of the bone that makes up his body.
I ask my friend if he knows this.
He laughs and says yes:
I've learned this, too.

IV.

When I think of the hub-cap turtle,
I now see a prayer wheel
spinning. And I know that
smattering of bone was a gift.
Look where it's led! To this
lost turtle-boy still in one piece.
To a woman, scarred and a little less lost,
dreaming through daylight of the way
that time spins away, the way
some pieces come together, the way
some people, crashing through life,
find their way back to the road
they travel, every loss and every wound
part of the air they breathe.

Which is not to say sentient creatures
didn't die—or that they won't.
Only that the living wind shushing
toward them and through them and away
has met all the plodding creatures
who traveled the road before them,
knows all the plodding creatures
who follow.

Sleep

Some whales sleep vertically, the bullet of their body
pointed toward the light—toward the ocean's surface
and the first breath of air they'll take on waking.

I've only just begun, again, to sleep through the night,
my body curled into itself, to the pulse of my heart,
to the rise and fall of my lungs. I and the whales,

taken together, serve as silent exclamation that the world
can wait. That light will be there when we need it.
That darkness, like the sea, has a rhythm of its own.

Abandon

after Will Scott's Abandoned Farmhouse

We collapse in the shade of what will outlast
us, the paths we made getting here already

rebounding. Ashes to ashes, they say, dust
to dust. All that sepia sadness nothing but

wilted memory. But gravel to grass—that slow
unfolding of life reclaiming itself—holds more

promise than the lapsed lines of our reaching
out, our trying to hold on. Look. See what rises

unruly, unholy, toward skies that hold no promise
being only what they are: empty space, vast

waiting. This is what you shall do—it's been said
before. Let go. Love the earth. Reclaim your life.

The Mechanics of Flight

The mosquitoes are feasting in Wellfleet,
mostly on me, fourteen bites on one uncovered arm
as I greet my host in the drive.
We've never seen anything like it, she tells me.
But I think of the birds
I came here to see, comfort myself thinking
they'll be feasting, too, this year, fat and happy
in the marshes, along the shore.

                    Later, at the sanctuary, I ask
the ladies in the welcome center—three times
before they understand me—if that thinking is right.
Much as that helps us, says one. *Small comfort,*
sniffs another. On the salt marsh trail,
air crisp with the scent of the sea, a red-winged blackbird
cries for my attention, flits and darts before landing
on the bridge before me. *See me?* he says.
Aren't I pretty? I laugh my way toward him
and he flies into the reeds, lands on a blade
so tall and fine I can't believe it supports his weight.
See what I can do? See? And when he's sure I have,
he flies to the top of a tree in the oak grove,
then, not satisfied, finds an even higher perch. *See how
high I can fly?* he says. *See me? See?*

But a blue-gray catbird has grumbled loudly, swooping
before me so my eye can't help but follow him
back to the reeds. I study his shape and sound, unsure
what he intends, but the red-winged blackbird
sings out shrilly. When I turn back to him, he's gone.
It's been a long day, but I know he means for me to follow
him, the only direction he could have gone: inward.

Deep in the grove, I spot an egret, holy, white,
alone. I gaze in stunned silence, while the split-tailed swallows
dive and dart

                          as if the scene were not exquisite enough.
I stare until I'm full, can feast no more, turn back
to the path I came from, marveling that I'd not felt
one mosquito bite all afternoon. Until one does, suddenly,
in the center of my right scapula, tiny thrust nudging me
to remember the vestiges of all my lives, the mechanics
of flight. That we all have wings or had them once.
That each feast is the same as every other.
That, here, we nourish one another.

Paula J. Lambert is a literary and visual artist from Ohio. Her full-length poetry collections include *The Ghost of Every Feathered Thing* (FutureCycle 2022); *How to See the World*, a finalist in the 2021 Ohioana Book Awards (Bottom Dog 2020); and *The Sudden Seduction of Gravity* (Full/Crescent 2012). She has also authored several chapbooks and is a literary translator. Awarded the 2021 PEN America - L'Engle Rahman Prize for Mentorship, Lambert's work has been supported by the Ohio Arts Council, the Greater Columbus Arts Council, and the Virginia Center for Creative Arts. She is the 2023 winner of the *Slippery Elm* Poetry Prize and the New England Poetry Club's Amy Lowell Prize, was awarded a 2021 Editor's Choice Award from *Sheila-Na-Gig online*, and was the 2019 winner of the Heartland Broadside Series. Lambert owns Full/Crescent Press, a small publisher of poetry books and broadsides, through which she has founded and supported numerous public readings and festivals that support the intersection of poetry and science, including the Sun & Moon Festival now hosted by the Ohio Poetry Association. She lives in Columbus with her husband, Dr. Michael Perkins, a philosopher and technologist. More at www.paulajlambert.com.

Sheila-Na-Gig Editions